Across The Open Glass Field.

Carys

Maloney.

DUSK BEFORE DAWN

Letters from The

Barrier

AND NOW

ACROSS THE OPEN

GLASS FiELD

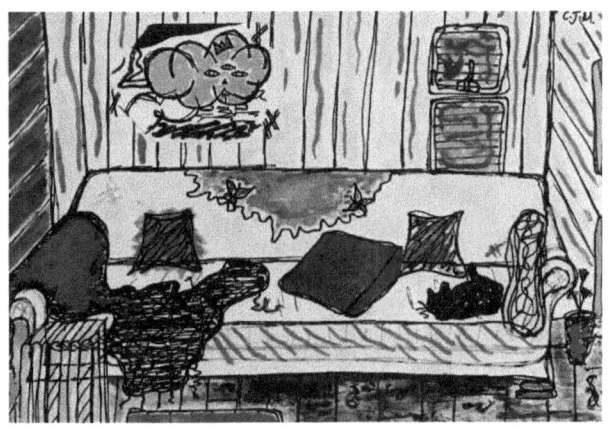

ISBN: 9798386837129

THIS IS

Not

(dot dot dot)

Do you mine the past

For inspiration—

Penetrate the present—

Look to the future to fill

Your cup? Do you circle

Yourself like a dropped

Pin, never quite finding

Your way in?

Are you feeling

A little bit conned?

CONTENTS

EXPANDED / AND SOME

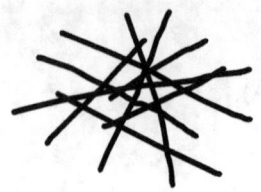

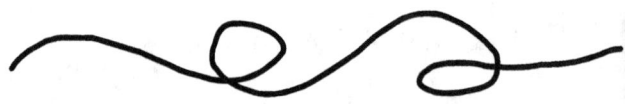

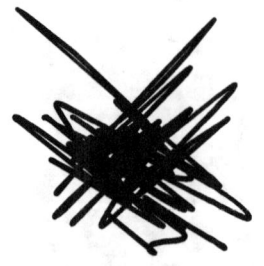

seemingly incongruous explosions

Carnaby Freaks (An Urban Meditation).

And with each year passing
(One here, another now)
I once believed myself to be moving
Further, away from you, yet this wasn't true
I grew, I grew—I circle home. I knew
Little of the nature of Time, I dipped
My fringes in the puzzles of Rhyme, or there
Where perplexing patterns are stitched.

Tell me, there's no need.
It's by paradox alone that we succeed—
The opposite approach shall work the most.
There are many things, only Time can teach
I want to know everything—sitting alone
On Carnaby Street, pervaded by gentrification
Sweeping the nation, Capitalist Feats—I search
The branded land, laced with an ugly nostalgia.
I won't find you here, nor will I find the past:
It's gone and dead, save The Stones Store
up ahead

Yet I'm filled with optimism for the future.
A future to fight for, despite
Everything against it. I think
Being human can be likened to one word:
Hope. And when Hope is forsaken,
Hell reigns in the heads of humanity.
I strive to mould my disparity
Into one harmonious whole,
Ever-giving, ever-bold, at least

It's a kind of bringing together—
I am as Eros to my flickering inclinations.

We the people
(One here, others now) passing
Here in Carnaby, well
We continue to live as best we can.
I fill my head with world literature and
Dwell, throw my soft glance upon
The art of the ages, in Silence, mourning
Yet giving new life. I tread the galleries as such:
Furtive funerals in each stare.
Eulogies resounding in my mind's eye,

As the children laugh
And turn the corner.

THE LONGING REBORE ITSELF AS
A NUCLEAR URGENCY—SO POTENT
IT BORDERED ON THE VIOLENT—
SHAKING MY SOUL BY THE SHOULDERS
ANY ILLUSION OF CHOICE
OBLITERATED
FOR BETTER AND FOR GOOD—
NO QUESTIONS ASKED
I RESOLVED TO LET IT POWER MY LIFE
VANDAL   VIOLENT   VITALITY
I'M ON AUTOPILOT   I'M JUST ALONG
FOR THE RIDE—
IT IS A FLOWERING OF MY FATE
A REFRAIN IN MY CHEST SCREAMING

NOW   NOW   NOW

                              I'M
              THROWN

    TO MY
                         FEET

                         I'M
         REACHING

         UP THE

                    WALL

Hollow Earth / Social (Media) Darwinism.

Is it someone's joke I was born so late?
Must I go on for my future's sake?
/
God is Dead
/
Digitalised capitalism the opium of the people
An urbanised nature draped in vape
A fast fashion stage of internet identities
/
We're all junkies, addicts with blue light
Bloodshot eyes, spurred onward
By vanity and infantile digressions
Bedazzled by the petty fantasy of ourselves
And all our anxiety, lugubrious notoriety
/
Heaven knows we've seen it all before
/
It's too much effort, this Real Life thing
Voracious and vicarious on Social Media
Beating time tit for tat with TV binges
I don't want meaning, I want pleasure
/
Why drag your belittled bones through Hell
until you're bare and barren, pure and open
barely breathing but born anew, a child
/
When you can get drunk, get high
Stay in, splash out
Make everybody love you
For an hour or two?

Forget forget forget me not
/
My Jäger shot TV junkie generation
Starving inaccessible excess
Culture feeds us empty calories
We devour, we feign satiety
/
Because it's scary to admit
We don't know what's missing
Because it's better to believe
That nothing is missing
&
Everything worth having comes
easy next day delivery guaranteed
orurmoneyback
/
Fuck your influencers
I carry my heroes in my head
I don't know if they're living or dead
/
Eloi everywhere I look / up from my phone
Social (Media) Darwinism
/
Man waves in his own destruction
A public display of unnatural camaraderie

Jeez, this poem is a drag

> *D'ya think it would*
> *sell better if I put it*
> *to music?*

Waterloo (Twenty-two Ten Twenty-two).

I am a Wim Wenders Angel
Sitting above Waterloo station.
Anything interesting today?

Ladies in plaid maid outfits
Emerging from the underground.
A waiting woman bearing a bouquet
Plaintive, hopeful. Heads bobbing with hats
Left luggage, long coats—the usual
Deadening rays of phone screens
Or windows into a higher existence.
Names and concepts are
Subject to change;
The needs of the mind
Remain the same.

I am a Wim Wenders Angel
Sitting above Waterloo station.
I told myself I'd catch an old movie;
Reconnect with something I love
So as to re-establish myself.
The mind can get murky, subject
To soaking up the world's clutter;
It's good to wipe the windows clean
From the inside, every now and then.
How do we establish balance
In a world of excess, a world
Of depravity? A wise man once said

Turn around and exhale. The Angel

Came to earth for love. Left Eternity
For colour and veins. It's amazing
What one's will can will;
Tracing the faces
Of the Berlin Wall.

I am a Wim Wenders Angel
Sitting above Waterloo station.
Repeating my words in different ways.
I'm gonna go catch that old movie;
Reconnect with myself
Wipe the windows clean
Before the sun again. Besides

It's good to leave Eternity for love;

(Even if you are a little late)

You will surely find

There isn't any difference

(This is what I tell myself).

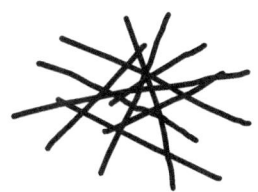

Freudian Drive-In.

Death, plastic and warm,
Moulds our every move.

Roses turn their backs.
Briefly red with futile rage,
So die with bowed heads.

In The Room With No Air
I fashioned lungs to speak
Your name—

Roses raise their chins.
Petalled mouths briefly parted,
So await your return.

Now I Understand Why the Pen Is Mightier
Than the Sword, Why Words Are Named as
Weapons.

Now I understand why the pen is mightier
Than the sword. He feared
My ink-tinged veins, the blood
I could spill with a single syllable. The tales
I could tell of Orwellian nights, of candlelight
& taking flight. The scenes
I could spin, Arachne-like,
Of perceived misgivings. He feared
The lair of my unpenetrated depths,
That which cannot be scoped:
The conjured-up lioness living there,
Chomping at the bit, hankering after
His reputation. I calmed his doubts:
I grant nothing more importance
Than it deserves; I act of my own accord.
And go about my business travelling lightly.

Now I understand why the word is named
A weapon. He feared
How I make letters curl
Under my nib, tame and purring
Submissive and instilled with
My Hera-like wrath. I calmed his doubts:
Ink is poisonous when injected, or ingested;
I told him of the truce I had made
So as not to die by my own hand.
I hold not to hatred for it stings the soul,

And makes a blunt épée of the sword
That is my attribute. I said his fear
Is unfounded: I do as I will, as I see fit.
I'll try everything, but only once (Temperance).
And reject not a thing that experience may bring.

Black   and   White
Are misperceptions / of sight.

I assured him: I live to trial, I live to learn.
I put Life on a pedestal, kneeling to worship
Her daily, through starving rumination and
Regret: they shall not know my name.
And the world, not yours.

                 (Long ago did I learn to let go
With the outward breath)

Now I understand why the pen is mightier
Than the sword, why words are named
As weapons. Nobody wants
Their ego immortally tainted
By a post-pubescent poetess.
But disregard your fear:
I am a warrior of justice, not of vengeance.
I hold no captive lioness, I embody
No chain-bound Greek goddess. As I said:
I worship Life only, I vowed to say yes
To every experience that stitches her seams,
Without discrimination. As I implied:

I am not a slave to soured emotion,
But a master of self-observation.
I regulate every move I make,
And watch as the world

Shifts accordingly. I am only learning
As the rest of us, as the best of us.
I step back and switch my glasses.
Turn to face the future with open limbs.

STRANGE
GIRL
DUG
FROM
PAST
EARTH

The Past Is a Blue-Tinged Motorway.

And I ride, and I ride. I curl my limbs and
place my face on the weeping window,
trace the heaven's teardrops of subdued
longing. I mimic, and I mimic well. And I hide
weary-eyed, a back seat basket case
by my side. Stuffed in like a shitty
stocking filler with so much baggage,
my sister bringing teddy bears to life
easing anticipated scenes. Back!
Crane my neck to check the faces
of cars with evil dagger eyes, chasing me
home like so many sheepdogs. Barking &
beeping. Swearing and swerving. Until

It's now, a ninety-degree turn toward
a gravel driveway, one day, one day,
I'll make my own way, you'll see, you'll pray
I'll slice open life, I'll mutilate my chains
with that metal kitchen knife, you'll see,
one day, I won't dream of running away,
I'll walk over that gravel driveway
like a ghost leaving her grave
for fleshy life, shedding my fear, one year,
one day, you'll see, you'll pray
but I'll be all gone, all free, always
with a burdened brain to twist the pain

into pretty shapes, my body too, my soul
shining lethal light antidote starter pack

make what you will, but make, but make
speak for her sake, speak in her wake
and ride over the blue-tinged motorway
on a cross-country train. Back!
Crane your neck to check the faces
of human beings with blue light eyes,
calling you home like so many sirens.
Turn and taste the sweet tears on the window.
They know your story, your future, your fate,
and they sing across the open glass field.

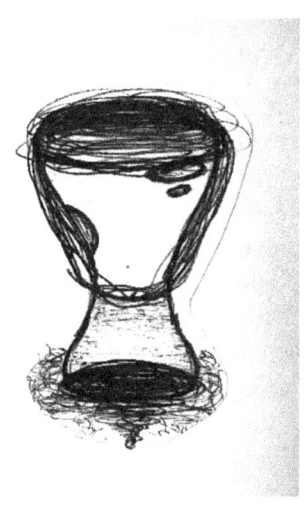

A Woman Alone.

Streets as wide as the Thames
Splayed with curling leaves.
Some newly dead, freshly fallen
Colourful corpses—others old-timers
Driven into wet tarmac; a grave for
A leaf. Falling. Flowing. Rotting.

Prime ministers come and go like
The seasons—clichés on change
Our daily existence. See,
It's eighteen degrees out
(Twenty-two by the hour hand);
Ten used to top a standard
October day, five years ago
Otherwise known as
The Days of Yore / or
Six iPhones ago.

Things change fast.
No one breathes
A word—the mild wind stirs me
To speak. The British flag bristles
Whilst we scoff at national pride
Put up a new storefront, decolonise.

Where are the people in St James's Park?
Does Nature lose her charms at night
Cinderella; is Nature a novelty

To the city? Does anyone else think
Like this? Look

Lovers on the bridge. I am a voyeur
I am David Bowie writing Heroes
In Hansa by the Wall.
Lovers Leaves. Lovers. Leave

Even the ducks wade and waddle in twos
Rippling along the river's skin,
Pecking at feathered derrières.
Geometric drains, plated coats of arms.
Art in the pavement to be stepped and shit on.
Art in the galleries to be silent before
Like God. People throwing tomato soup
At Nature-loving Vincent
To save the Earth

There must be a better way.
The Strand seats the arses of the humble
And suddenly there's a palace, a white sky,
A king

A man
Walks by. I picture him
Asking me: a woman alone
At this hour. The sun
My lover my counter my protector
Gone. Silent, he passes by.
To his back, I speak my reply:

I'm more afraid
  of not living
    than of dying.

What choice do I have
But to go on? Out of my sight,
I wonder if he understands.

I am a Woman <u>I am</u>
A writer what do you
Say to that ?

not much

FEMME FATALE

~~FEMALE~~ FLÂNEUR

Living.

The ticket man
Had your voice.
He told me
Where to go;
I didn't ask
I'm grateful anyway.
This is the height of
My social interaction;
A week without work
In London. I'm Lana
Alone on a Friday night;
The cinema with
The concertina ceiling.

Actress in this movie
Sat at table next to mine
Summer; strained to hear
Her conversation about
Moving house old friends
Wealth. How did she get
Inside the silver screen?
I don't know. But I'm going
To follow her. Blast off
In this concertina chair
From Lang's Metropolis
To the Promised Land.

Saturday Service.

Amber leaves flicker like
Mosaics shaking off
The light. The rain
Is laced with protest.
Enlivens the humans
Lining the Northbank.
Handing out papers singing
Songs loving neighbours.
Umbrella sea of solidarity
Shifts from sole to sole
Queasily. "Britain is Broken"
And outrage unspoken
Breaks over the banks
Of the Thames.

Effacing churchman,
His grim-faced ladies.
A woman walks in,
Glimpses the gold leaf
Byzantines, is told
To pay up or leave.
Even God Himself is a commodity
Under the Command of Capitalism.
See, they stitched a tag
To the Big Guy's beard
Stuck his salesperson
In a Ruby Red Robe
And told him
To proclaim
Unto his children:

That'll be thirty pounds
(Twenty-eight concessions)
To trample the marble graves
Of Royalty. And hey, you!
Breathing Poet! Only dead wordsmiths
Past this point. Join the queue
And you'll be with them soon.

Back to the street with
My weather-beaten
Bulgakov, back to the living
Reading the dead, back to divinity
In clouds of outward breath.
Frisky squirrels and flying ducks.
I find my faith
In the creatures
Here below.

Creatures who act, creatures who speak.
Creatures who cry and protest for peace.
Creatures who bring the warmth
Of Heaven back (under the eyes
Of the Metropolitan Police),
From frozen floors
From flimsy tealights
To the rain-strewn streets
Of heady hope.
To the hearts of the people
Who belong there
The most.

———————INCIPIT ZARA

if you Tell YOUR TRUTH

YOU ARE A PREACHER

(RIDICULED / REPENTANT)

IN AN Atheist AGE / oF

a t o m i s a t i o n ———————

THUSTRA

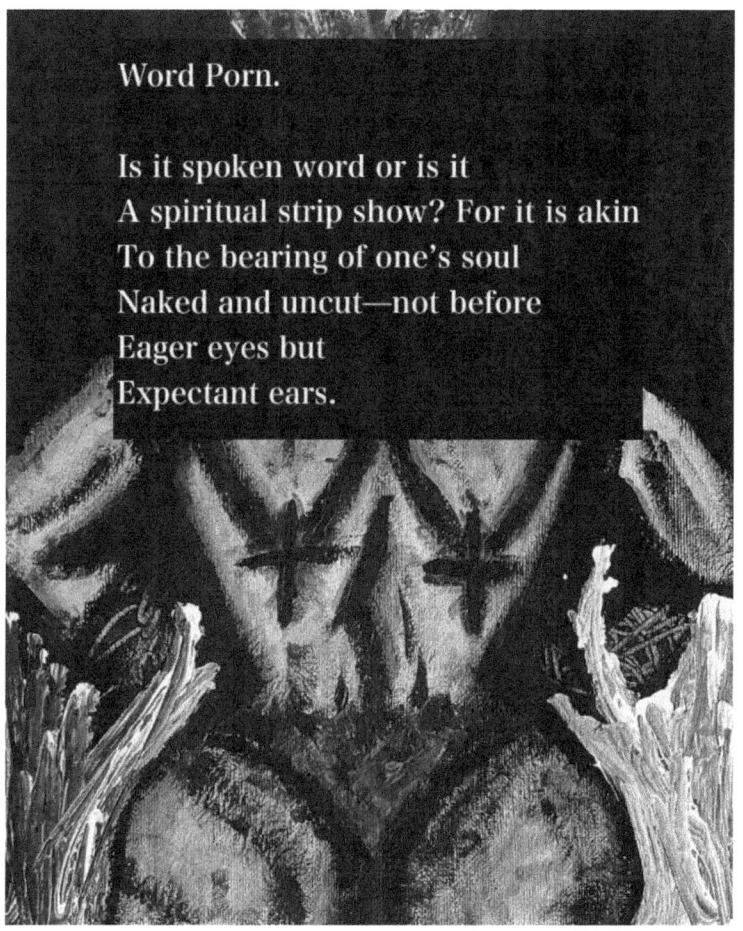

Word Porn.

Is it spoken word or is it
A spiritual strip show? For it is akin
To the bearing of one's soul
Naked and uncut—not before
Eager eyes but
Expectant ears.

Writ on the Morn of My 21st Birthday.

Woke up early like a Christmas kid
Scrubbed my face on a bus to London

I remember gliding over the M40. The sunlight
split the trees, stripped the road.
Golden Dawn. You could've fried an egg
on those streets. The sun spots
Dabbed themselves onto tarmac
like bingo markers (my numbers are 777)
This was my last morning—

Did I have you fooled? Evening past,
I opened a small box:
Inside, a key, enclosed. For me.
Something revealed—at least
Hinted at. I'm only a year older
Yet I'm sensing the revelation
that stuns the elderly, or
the waning with Youthful Hearts:
the exposing of all clichés as truth
or the handbook as hiding in plain sight.

Could it be?
An oyster, a pearl? (my birthstone is pearl)
Something is opening itself, anyhow—
a kind of mellow burning, a nuclear flower plant
unfurling, hot like

The day I was born.
And resistance as violence is dead to me.

It comes to me in moments   holding you
dear   in my peripheral   imminent
spreading you   over   my senses   like those
slippery sunbeams   Heaven   is then   when
I feel you so near in   my mind   buzzing   alive
alive   and we are   whole   It comes   to me
then   in an   instant   then   I know
things to be   as they   truly are   I know   all
is well   why I am   and what   I was   to you
Then we   are   everything   and truer than
true   In moments
does it   come to
me

Toi

Toi

Toi

White lines
On the road.
Sober and drunk
In equal measure.

Could it be
That this is the world?
I have forsaken
Thought. I am sure.
I feel so sure. I feel I understand
Just a bit more. Just enough

This time. Enough to get by
(my birth sign is Cancer and 3 is my time)
I remember gliding over the motorway
a vehicular trance—I remember
that sun-speckled morning like an egg blackened
on the hard shoulder stove—I remember
my 21st year awakening with
the Sunny Side Up

give us a
SMILE,
love

OUR TOLERA-
NCE IS
TOO HIGH

ASTRONOMI-
CALLY APath
etiC

BLASÉ BOURGEOISIE

BB

Born Blue.

Born. Blue
Strangled, new
Tumbling, smiling
Crying, crapping
Hiding. What
I was seeking
I did not know.

Flung to my feet and
Dancing with butterflies
In my belly, falling short
Of breath, walking the four
Inch plank of perfection.
My hands are bleeding.
I need to piss.
I hope I get a lollipop
After this.

What if he turns up here
Loud, bare-chested
Calling out my name?

All hope to the future!
Like the eggs in one basket
Like the pot at the rainbow's end
Like the temptress tempting one to bed.

fear never freedom
fear never freedom

more alive before
i came here
we all must pass through
or something like that. - - -

School bell sounds and I'm scared
Of going, scared of leaving, scared
Of loud music and crashing drawers.
What about this world inside me?
I come with a past yet I'm scolded
Like a child. If this is a fresh page
Make it a pretty one.
I am dependent on a nuclear bomb.

uncertainty never safety
uncertainty never safety
pack up and leave
at sundown

grab your toys
seal your lips
turn up at school
and excel

purgatory is
a living hell. some things
a child should never tell. - - -

Mid-teens, full of dreams
Divorce settlements
Heinz Baked Beans. Working hard
Getting lonely—life's less now
But a little gone off. I guess
I'm doing quite well—

A normal life, kinda swell
Friends. Holidays. Bottle Green Blazers.
Is there somewhere else
I need to be? I sleep these days
Tired after training—
A resting curly head
In a quiet house. Paradise
Never looked so nice.

Headlines. They mean nothing yet
Head in a case of infantile regret
I graduate, I get on a jet
I start anew, fall black and blue
With box-dyed hair to match.
Dark. I don't want it—
Anything but the mundane
A slippery slope, a tightening of chains
Something must shift.
Something must change.
I'm leaving the line
That tows the masses
To their graves. Bid farewell.
Jump and pray. - - -

The eighth day, and the world has begun.
I find it empty, for you've been and gone.
Understanding comes in stages
But truth comes at once.
I had so much to learn,
I have so much to become.

If my past ghost was flung
Into the present she'd scream
An Ode to Joy. No such transition

Can occur: Real Life is much
Too subtle. Change comes
And we change with change.
We cease to identify with
Our forsaken skins. We are new
Born again with each shift
Of life's bowels. What came before
Is as good as never happened.

I'm safe now. I am alive
I never lived to see my childhood
Thrive, The Three Fates, they said otherwise.

I sighed
my
primordial
sigh

I am not the same as I was. - - -

The eighth day, and the world has begun.
I find it empty, for you've been and gone—
But I am here
And that is something.
Yes, I am here
And that is something.

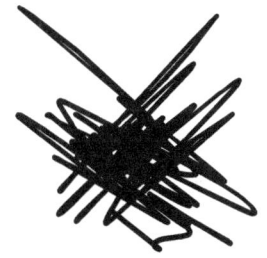

Ryanair Prayer.

Blue moon beasts.
Symmetrical city severs the clouds
Man-made light for an airplane's flight.
Collapsing territories.
The plane a puppy's belly.
Piercing lands lesser leant toward
Tumble into view. The crux of you
Bleeding into bodies new
Descending awe, wistful, over muted life.

I am reminded of what it means
To snap my bones in a self-destructing age.
To turn the page, to give oneself over
To pray in the pews of an economy aircraft.

Cala Major (A Sharing of Initials).

There,
Where the world is slow.
The people come and go
(Inebriated tidal waves)
To escape their spheres
Of creation. Me,
I'm here to clear
The vitrine of my vision—
Smeared, somewhat
From a city's clouding
Temperament.

My sphere, it forms around me
Of me, through me.
I do not create: I channel.
I do not wait: I am present.
May it be known, by all
That these things be
Sufficient.

Insomnia.

Insomnia. The moon moves fast
About my window; a charcoal sky
Her reluctant companion.
These are the nights between
The days in waiting. Still,
Life demands to be lived;
A pledge to the present as ever enough.

I see the signs as I see everything else:
As fully as possible, and without fear.
To become unmoved, one must first
Become aware
Of the signs, that once were
Perceived—infallible

Omnipotent. I know better now.
I see the signs as I see everything else
I cannot be deterred. Words burst
Their seams. Moon behind the gutter;

Fine, let those who find rest have it.
These are the days that bind
The nights in waiting. Still,
Sleep stalks her prey, scopes
The joint, lacks
The courage needed to kill. Insomnia

Addiction Apparition (AA).

Grief is the thing with daggers,
Severing the strings of Time's Vile Bow
With a longing unprecedented.

Being small and having
An addict parent
Hovering over you
Like an apparition.
All darkness light gone out
Not really human.
There in body
Not in soul. Strange
Scary scarce smile
I would search within
Try to fish you out
Of black death seas.
No bait was stronger
Than the waters you
Drowned in. I remember
Red lights and
Rehab units. Night
And day. Home
Or away. Searching
The cityscape and
Listening for sirens
Or slamming doors.
Hushed whispers or
Whimpers behind

Smeared glass. Small
And having an addict
Not a parent stabbing
Hope through the heart
Not helping with
Homework. Spiritual death
Like Prometheus inviting the eagle
Back to feast each night
Futile sacrifice. No gods
Condemned you. I learnt
Today that you never
Wanted children so as
Not to pass on generational
Trauma like some plague
Black death seas.
Drowning every night
Groundhog Day of Fear
Alright. Like Prometheus
Pecking out his own liver
Chained to the rock. The rock
The addict parent is not
To the small child who
Is similar in spirit silenced
By swear words secrets
Sent to gymnasium halls
To perform under pressure
Too heavy for a child to
Withstand on their hands.

Everything is upside down.
Why won't the world wake up?

I learnt today how
You laughed and
You danced
On the other side
Of the world
And I sobbed into
The winter night.

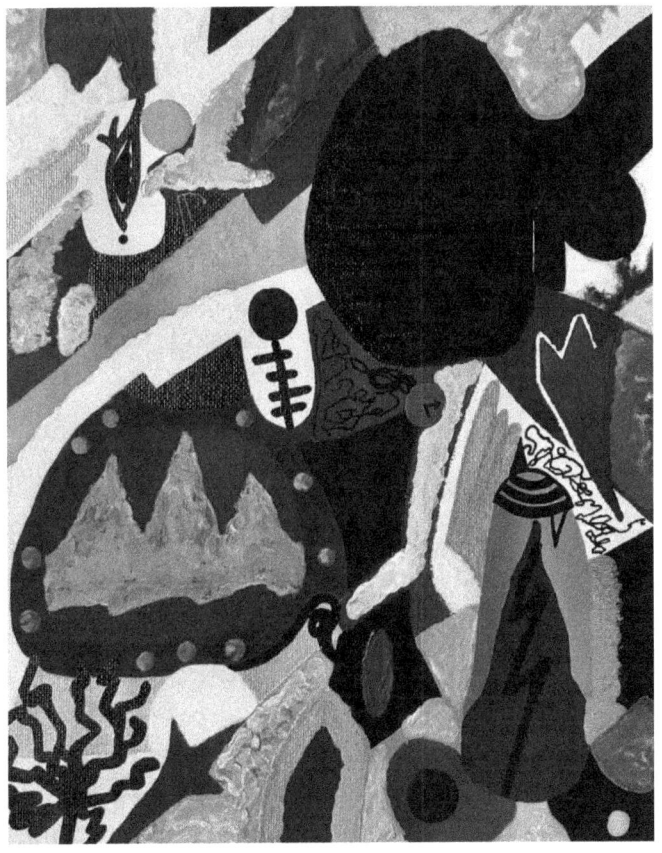

SOCIETY SAYS:

THE FeMALE EQUIVALeNT

oF the

tortured   artistic

genius Type

is THE

crazy   fucking

bitch Type

//

Daedalus Aloft Despite.

I am a Poet I am not
A sculptor. I let life mould me
That which gave me form
In the first place. Open! Open!
Open! Disregard the self and see
How wide life can be. There is nothing
In the way there is nothing
To be feared. Get with your body
Sink down in your heart place, rest.
Sleep a waking reverie. Know the passing
Of wind under wings bound for the sun,
A world untainted by interpretation.

Love is the root of all form love
Cannot be killed. Love can only be
Given back to itself, with greater intensity
Than before, singing of certitude
And corporeal adventure. Let love
Leak down your cheeks. Carry each loss
In your heart. Live as the one you grieve for.

WHETHER YOU KNOW
it OR   NOT

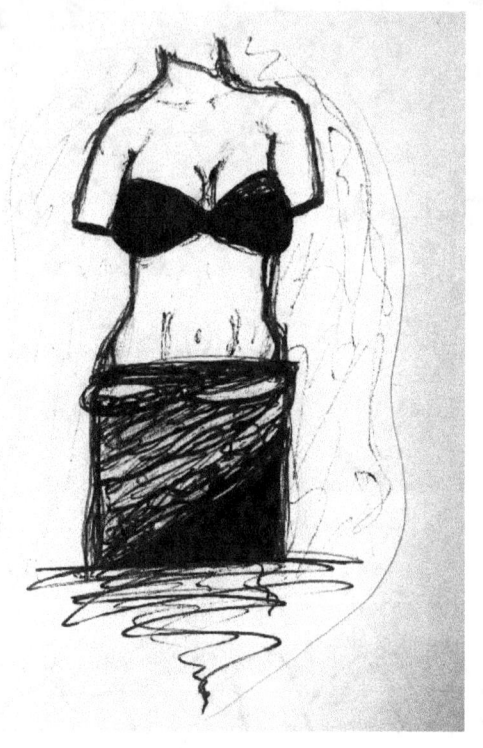

We are taking
a very new shape

the words are
drugged and worn
and all
that I have
left

AND

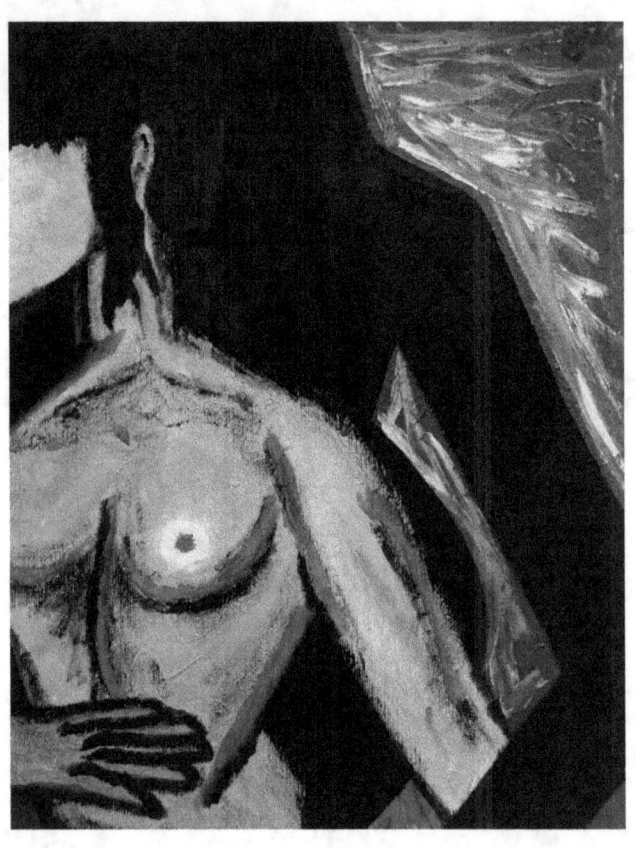

SOME

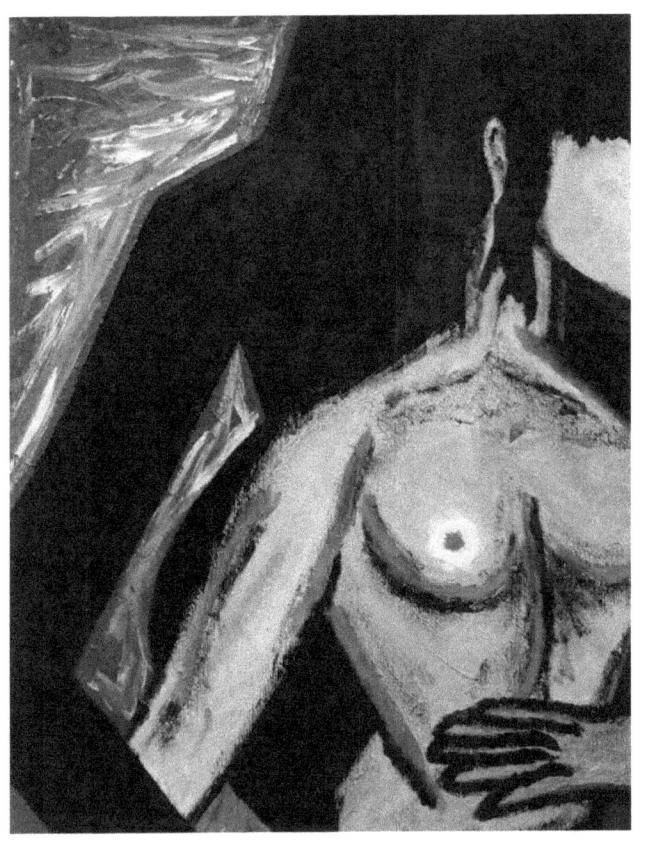

Selene and Endymion (A Song).

I'm big, and I'm brave
Out in the world
Oh, you should see me
How I wish that you could see me
How I wish that you could be me

I'm big, and I'm brave
Out in the world
And I hope, that you'd be proud of me

But I'm grieving, I'm grieving
And I know I'll go on grieving
For the rest of my days
Because

My body, it is warm
And it wants to know yours
My flesh, it is real
And it wants to feel yours

And I can't, and I won't
Oh, I'll love you, all the same
How I'll love you, all the same
How my joy is worth my pain

And I can't, and I won't
And I'll wake up every day

Big and brave
Out in the world
My love is living
My life has unfurled

But my soul, it is searching
The blind man in the dark
It doesn't understand
Where you've gone

It doesn't understand
For my soul, it is searching
And it doesn't understand
Where you've gone

Selene and Endymion
Selene and Endymion
Selene and Endymion

It doesn't understand
Where you've gone

Requiem for R.J.E.

Hypocrisy is my policy
Irony, my philosophy
I lace my meaning with double wit

My heart is a bloodied pomegranate
Deflowered, devoured, digested,
Defecated; seeds planted sprouted
Some mirror, cracking up real wise
 Before my presence.

Demons declare their
Blemished breeding ground
Within the brains of angels

The ugliness of humanity's
Juvenihilistic ignorance
Huffs its gallows-hung guffaw
(All cruelty / callousness)
Upon the sound of sight

Evasion is perversion
And we love to put it off
It's such a heinous affair

Satyrs, their satanic spawn
Parade in the satire-sitcom
Of Mankind's Modernity
Patrol the pure of heart

Preach misunderstanding
Fetishise the Vegetative State
For Capitalist Garrulous Gain

Of late. Citizens suck pacified
On sugar-coated superficiality
And Lord, we learnt to recycle.

M i - s h e e - m a h

Flecks of feathers
Stubbed out cigarettes
Forever circumambulate
Truth-telling necks

Subtle areas of twisted repetition
I picked up a shard and saw myself

Demons don't discriminate.
They devour their kind
Their kingdom
Their host

Nothing remains.
And there you are
The Black Reset that
Wakes an Overdose

What is left
Is what knows Peace
Alone

Enduring angel
I think you are
Where Dante ended up.

GREAT ART SHOWS
THE WORLD Its
OWN SULLIED
FACE ★★★☆

Baby Cries Why.

Daddy got no money
He spent it all on drink
Mama got no work
Stress made her take it sick

Crashing cars and scaling bars
Tending patients in the wards
Obsessive neurotic need for control
Punched even digits in phone dials

And baby cries why, baby cries why
Frosty Jack bottles, Jack Frost rhymes
Cry baby why? Why baby cry?

Bunches and braids
Petticoats and plaid
One to ten three times.

Daddy got a honey
He keeps her in a jar
Visits her on PC screens
Pretends she ain't so far

Mama got a secret
A code for crisis days
Authority and discipline
So baby knows the way

And baby cries why, baby cries why
Frosty Jack bottles, Jack Frost rhymes
Cry baby why? Why baby cry?

Bunches and braids
Petticoats and plaid
One to ten three times.

Boo-hoo baby, stuck-up sour
Kisser of lies, visage so dour
Baby why broken?
Shaken not spoken

Doesn't know where to begin /
Decides to scream for an end

And baby cries why, baby cries why
Frosty Jack bottles, Jack Frost rhymes
Cry baby why? Why baby cry?

Bunches and braids
Petticoats and plaid
One to ten three times.

Allusions.

The imprint of lips on
Burgundy coffee cups.
Rain is lustre glazing
Atop the street
A layer of lacquer
Reflecting the sky
Back to itself.
Sky notices.
Clouds over
With disbelief.
A war is waged
Between wind
And cigarette.
A bitter flicker
Then sodden
Trodden
Ash.

You opened up my Heart
To the deeper reality
Of Sight.
I would not be here
Without you.
You lifted the lid
Of Pandora's box
Stepped back
And watched
As light-years
Of love
Of longing

Resolved themselves
In Peace
Steeped
In a
Trailblaze
Of tears.

You, who did this
I, who did this
We, who are this
Healing and furthering each other as
A mutilated flower
Repairs itself and stretches
Blindly toward
The sun. That's us—
Gormley's figures
On terraced rooftops.
Nighthawks haunting
Hopper's city corners.
Forever waiting
To touch.
Who could know?
How we
Inwardly rejoice
Surrendering
Inexplicable
Certainty.

Your image
Is held
In my mind
Like God.

Ever-born
In the womb
Of thought.

The imprint of lips on
Burgundy coffee cups.
Rain is lustre glazing
Atop the street
A layer of lacquer
Reflecting the sky
Back to itself.
Sky notices.
Clouds over
With disbelief.
A war is waged
Between wind
And cigarette.
A bitter flicker
Then sodden
Trodden
Ash.

I sink back home
And find you
Warm.
Humming
Toward
Parading
Flames
Spitting
From our
Fireplace.
I kiss your face
And tangle your

Hair. Softly
I affirm your
Flesh. Pray
For the day
When I live
To see
The Internal
And External
Resolve themselves
In Peace.

I see you
Before
You lock
The lid.
Truth made
Visible
Within
Your eyes.
And it's dark
Warm
Just like
The womb
Before the
Thunderbolt.
And there's   you
Humming
Songs eternal
Toward our
Spitting
Fireplace.
Home. I sink
Toward the
Start. My

~~We are only this:~~
~~The sun and moon at night.~~
~~You cannot be seen~~
~~I reflect your light.~~

Toe, tracing
The finish line.

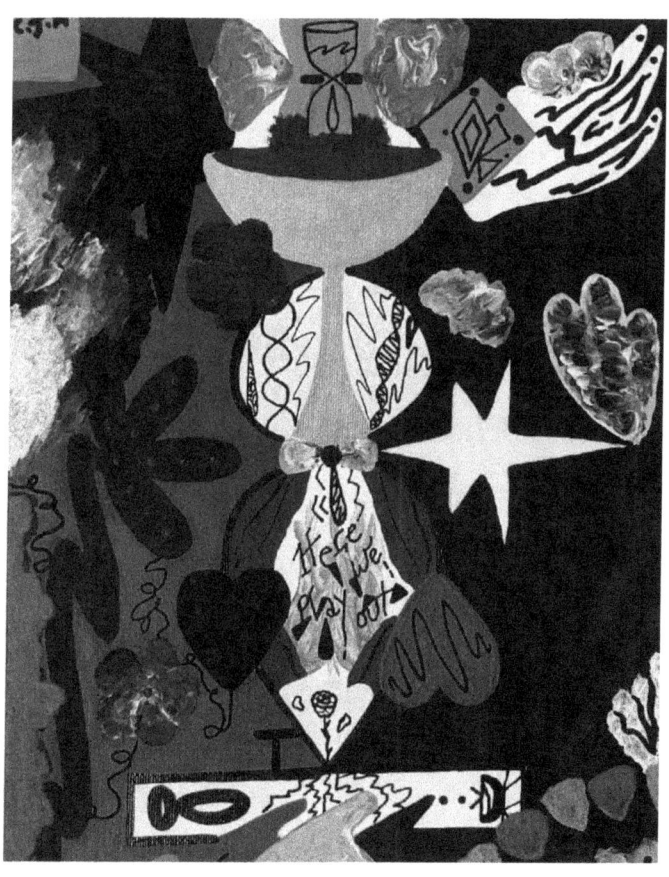

The Farmhouse.

Rolling fields of lavender run
Ample, toward the horizon, toward
The farmhouse where you played alone
Innocent, as a boy, in my dream.

I know not more—even then
You seemed to be missing something
Integral—something childhood
Could not grant you. How you pleaded!
Coal mines behind brilliant black eyes.
Receptive, but not yet receiving.

Some Vague Gesture.

Softness is the greatest strength.
It is defiance in the face of a callous world;
It is to scoff at the shallow state of
Bitterness. It is not
Lying down to be trampled by vice.
It is pure confidence in knowing
You cannot be harmed.

Walls preserve life
At the expense of experiencing it.
They say to bleed is to be alive;
The world wraps itself in bandages
Mummified, playing dead, breeding
Numbness.
Swatting pain like a bluebottle.

I fear no one
Will understand my meaning. It is only
To grasp the gist of some vague gesture.

Reprise: Across The Open Glass Field.

Among the recent days,
Unearthing pale traces of you.
Forever in flashes of green;
Fresh faces spark my way home.

Two thousand roses wither and die
in the scramble for time. Pennies
and clovers are crushed underfoot.
Crimson roses. Green clovers. Trains
on tracks and people in trains of
chugging mind games. Dumb dead
flâneur observational poem piece
*   ends book.*

blackout poetry

masterwork

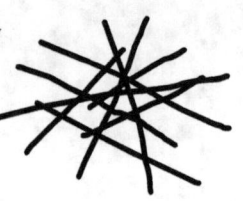

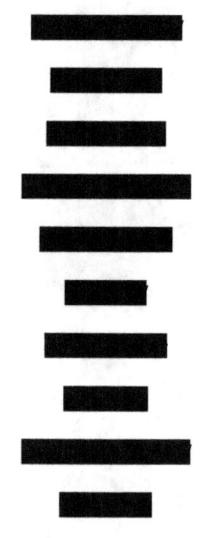

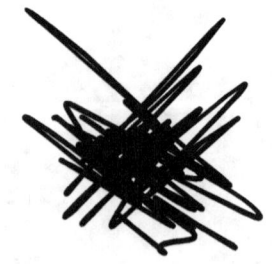

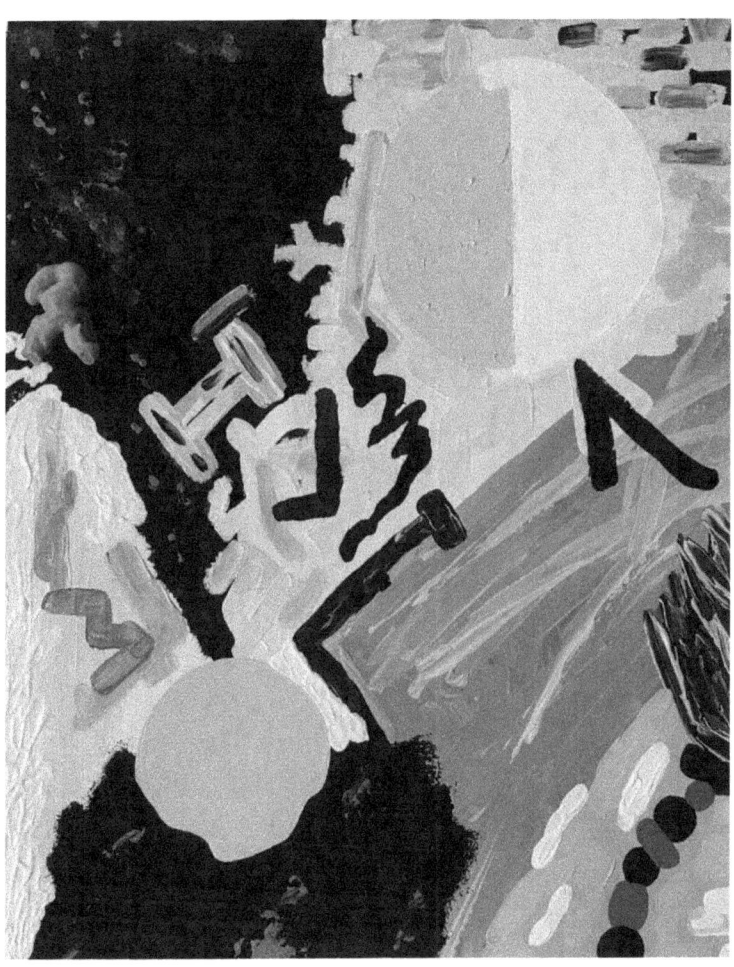

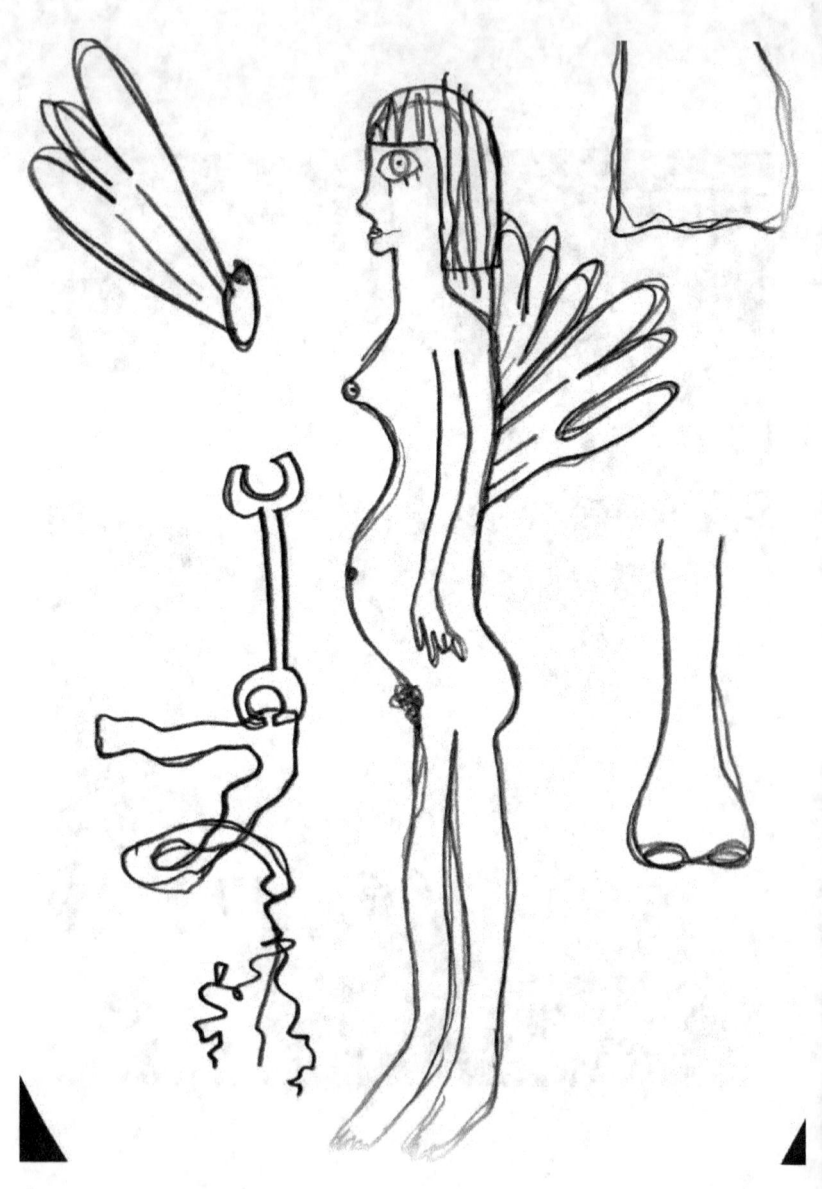

through every
dwindled
2020 desire
unrealised
I feel ~~that~~ I have
lived and died
One thousand lifetimes
Without ever drawing
breath

Carys Maloney